MARY LEAF
A Leaf Collection

BOOK 1

Notes from the Publisher

Composers In Focus is a series of original piano collections celebrating the creative artistry of contemporary composers. It is through the work of these composers that the piano teaching repertoire is enlarged and enhanced.

It is my hope that students, teachers, and all others who experience this music will be enriched and inspired.

Frank J. Hackinson

Frank J. Hackinson, Publisher

Notes from the Composer

When our children were small, I would take them for walks where we would pick up brightly colored leaves, pine cones, interesting rocks, twigs, and anything else that constituted a "treasure." Then we would take all our treasures home , and make collages out of them on large pieces of paper. *A Leaf Collection* is an assortment of different things – pieces about different seasons, about different ethnic groups, about different experiences, about different historical events – and it reminded me of the collages that we used to make. My hope is that children of all ages will enjoy the musical journey of these pieces as much as I enjoyed writing them!

Best wishes,

Mary Leaf

Mary Leaf

Contents

Ancient People

*Ancient people called the Anasazi lived around 2,000 years ago and are thought to be the
ancestors of Indian tribes such as the Hopi, the Zuni, and the Pueblo. They lived in the
Four Corners region of New Mexico, Colorado, Utah, and Arizona.*

Mary Leaf

Steadily (♩ = ca. 108)

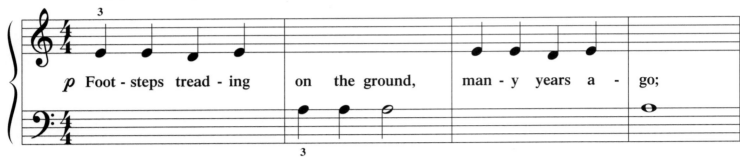

Foot - steps tread - ing on the ground, man - y years a - go;

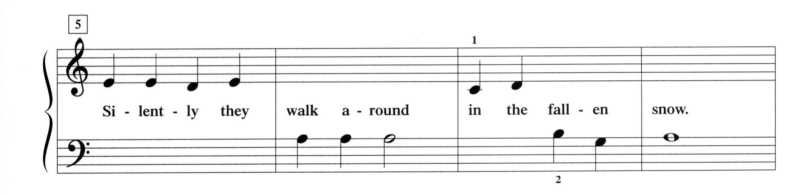

Si - lent - ly they walk a - round in the fall - en snow.

Teacher Duet: (Student plays 1 octave higher)

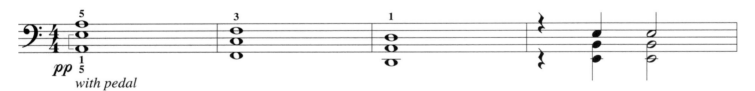

pp *with pedal*

In the Glen

Joyfully (♩. = 76-84)

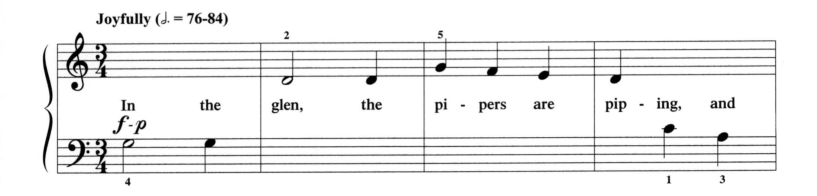

In the glen, the pi - pers are pip - ing, and

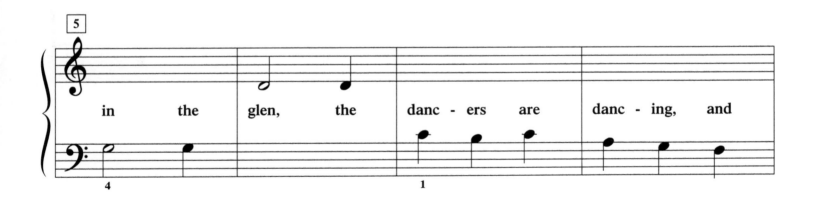

in the glen, the danc - ers are danc - ing, and

Teacher Duet: (Student plays 1 octave higher)

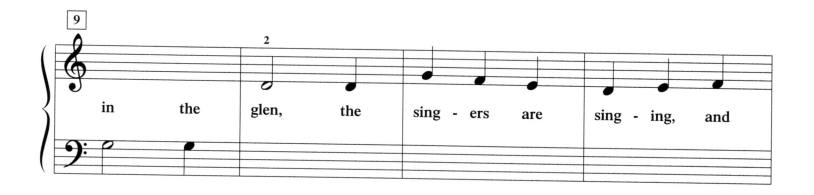

in the glen, the sing - ers are sing - ing, and

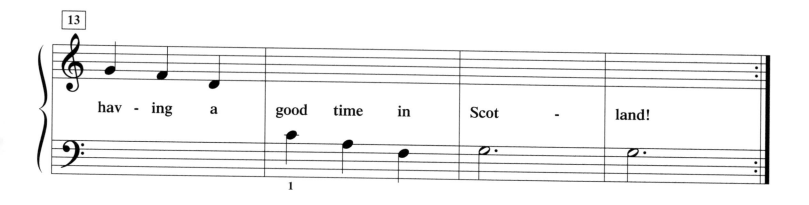

hav - ing a good time in Scot - land!

for my grandniece, Maggie Leaf

Raindrops On Our Path

Lightly; steadily (♩ = ca. 100)

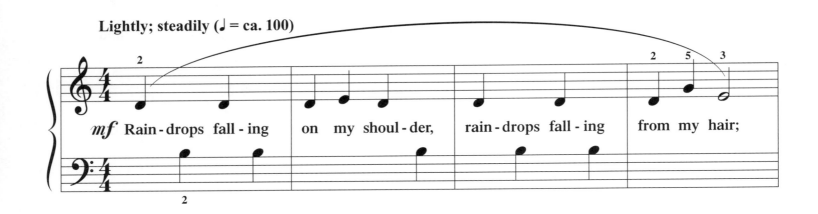

mf Rain-drops fall-ing | on my shoul-der, | rain-drops fall-ing | from my hair;

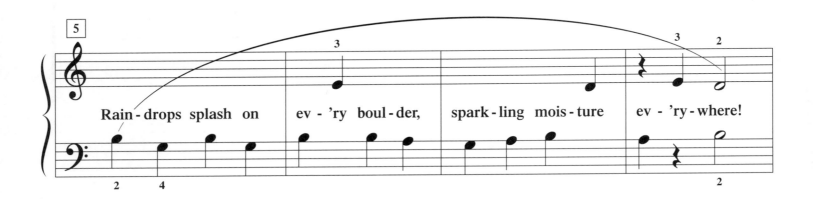

Rain-drops splash on | ev-'ry boul-der, | spark-ling mois-ture | ev-'ry-where!

Teacher Duet: (Student plays 2 octaves higher)

Rain-drops on our path de-scend-ing, spread a mist up - on the way;

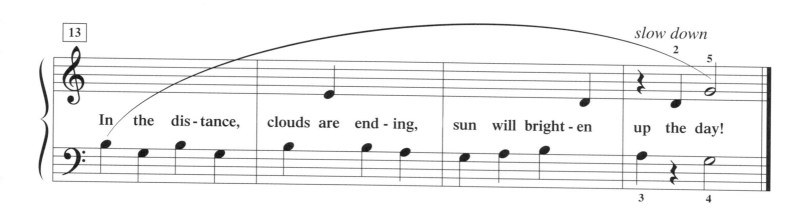

slow down

In the dis-tance, clouds are end-ing, sun will bright-en up the day!

rit.

Crazy Horse

In 1948, a mountain sculpture was begun in the Black Hills of South Dakota to honor a hero of American Indians — Crazy Horse. Crazy Horse Mountain stands as a tribute to the original inhabitants of America, and is still in the sculpting process.

Steadily (♩ = ca. 132)

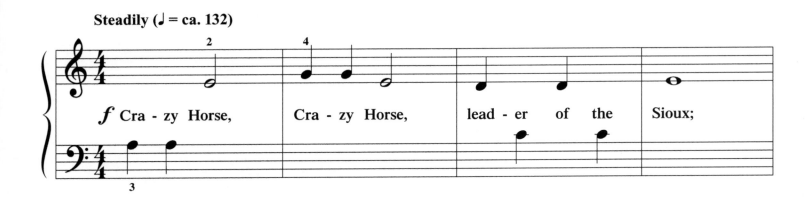

f Cra - zy Horse,   Cra - zy Horse,   lead - er   of   the   Sioux;

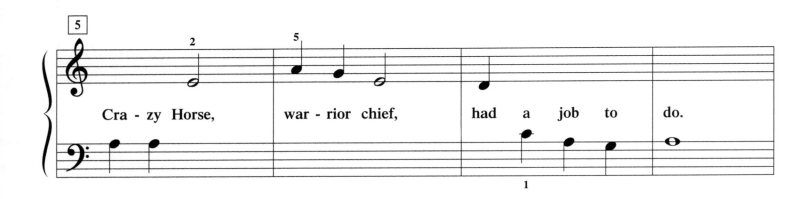

Cra - zy Horse,   war - rior chief,   had   a   job   to   do.

Teacher Duet: (Student plays 1 octave higher)

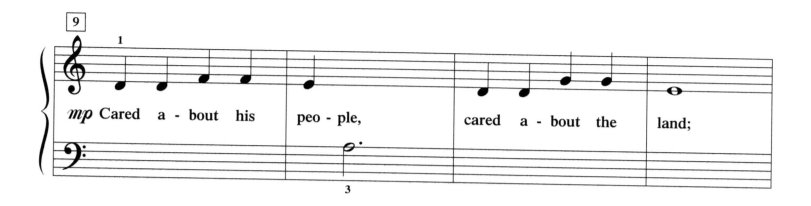

Optional lyric for Verse 2

Crazy Horse, Crazy Horse, leader of the Sioux,
Crazy Horse, you've a great mountain named for you!
Riding on your pony, pointing at your land,
Crazy Horse, warrior chief of your fighting band!

FF1713

Summer Haze

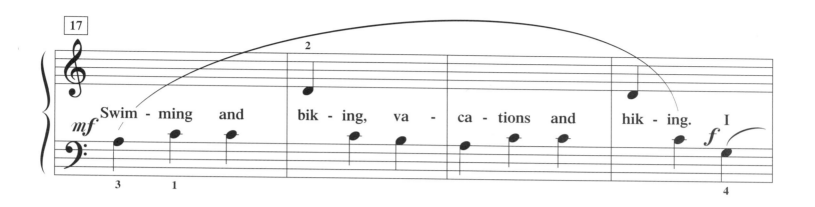

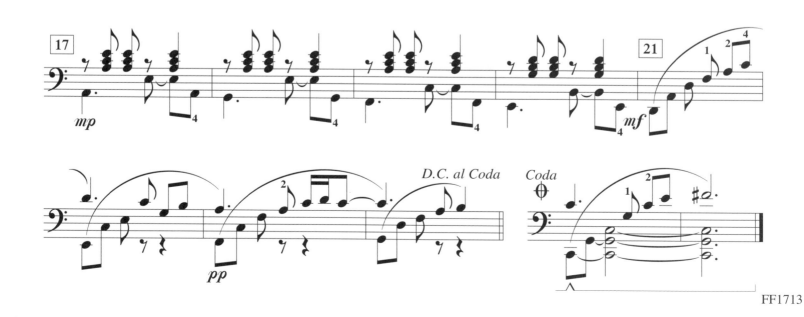

School Days

Happily (♩ = ca. 168)

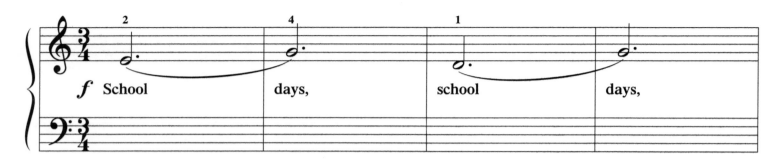

f School days, school days,

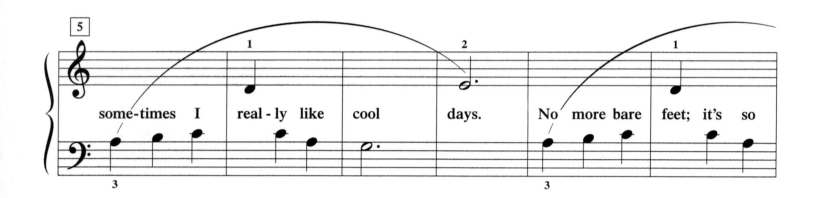

some-times I real-ly like cool days. No more bare feet; it's so

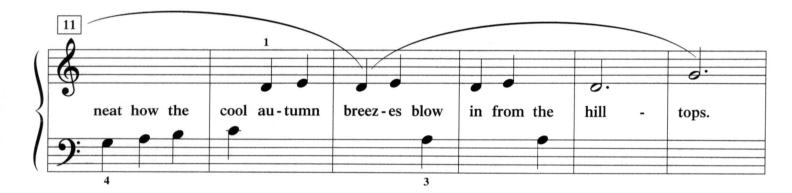

neat how the cool au-tumn breez-es blow in from the hill - tops.

Teacher Duet: (Student plays 1 octave higher)

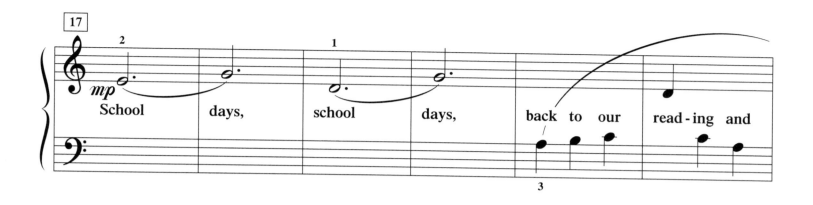

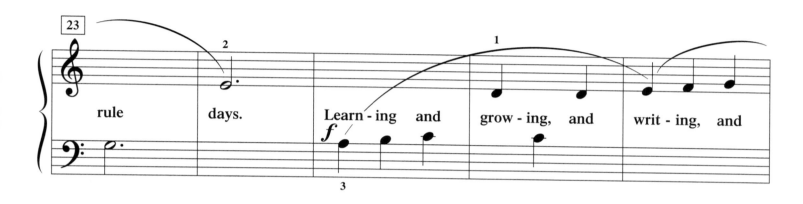

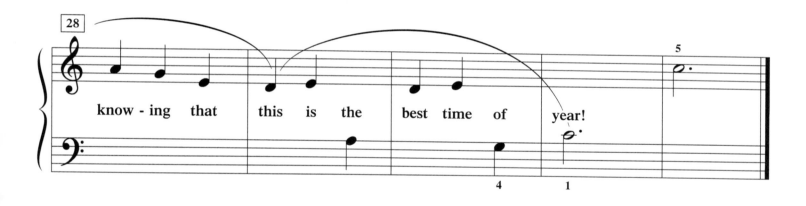

A Pirate's Life

Swashbuckling! ($\quad$ = ca. 100)

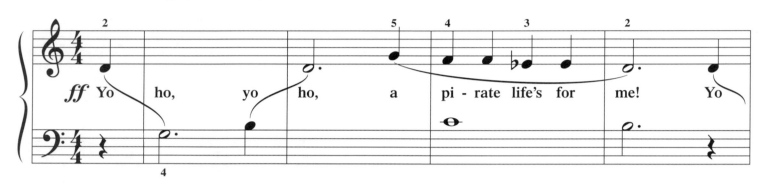

Yo ho, yo ho, a pi - rate life's for me! Yo

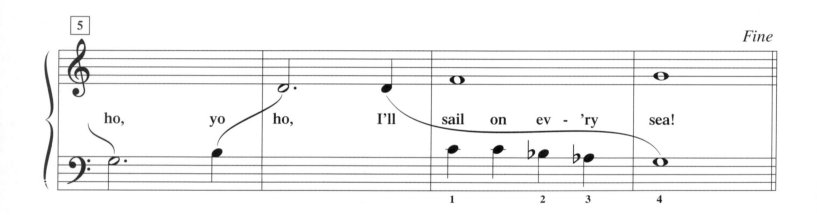

ho, yo ho, I'll sail on ev - 'ry sea!

Fine

Teacher Duet: (Student plays 1 octave higher)

Fine

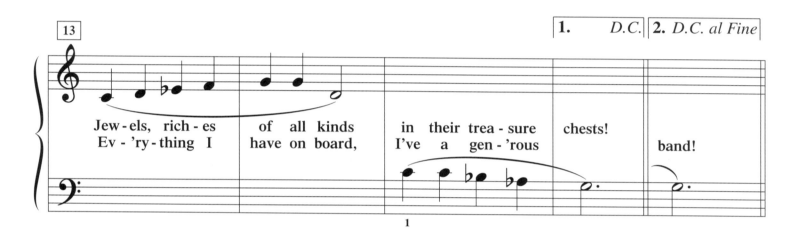

First Snow of Winter

Slowly and thoughtfully (♩ = ca. 80)

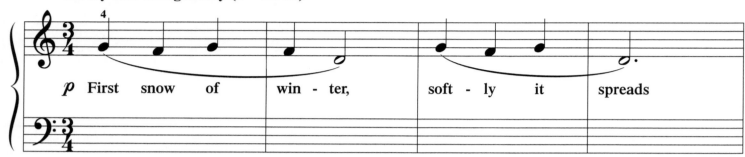

p First snow of win - ter, soft - ly it spreads

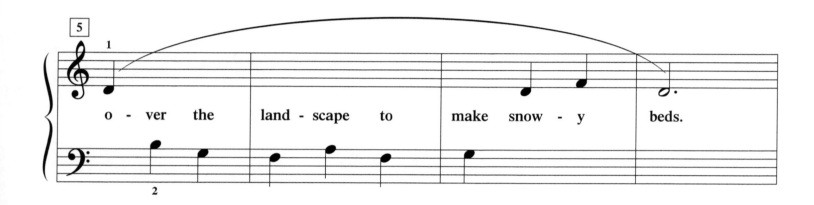

o - ver the land - scape to make snow - y beds.

Teacher Duet: (Student plays 1 octave higher)

pp
with pedal

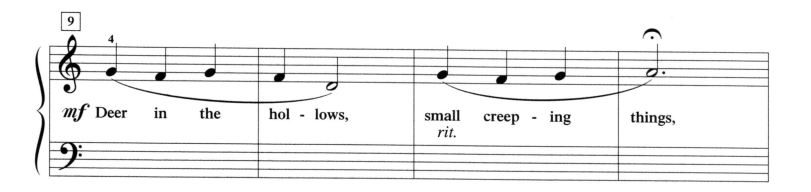

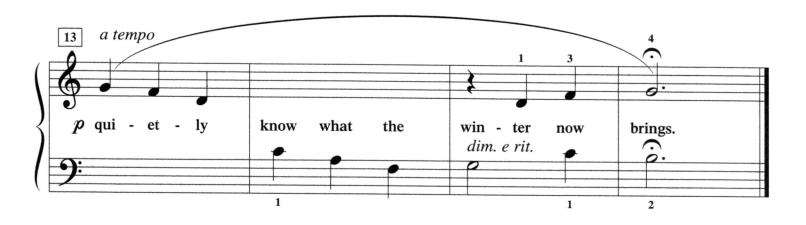

Time to Boogie!

With energy! ($\downarrow$ = 92-100)

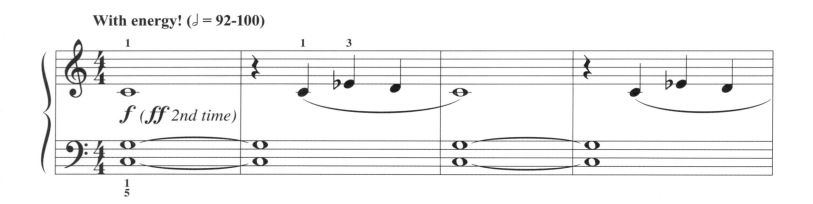

f (**ff** 2nd time)

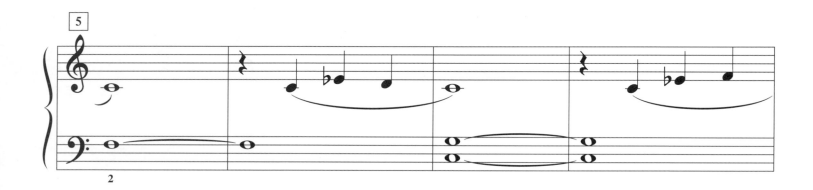

Teacher Duet: (Student plays 1 octave higher)

L.H.

mf (**f** 2nd time)

Autumn Leaves Are Falling

Flowing gently (♩ = ca. 100)

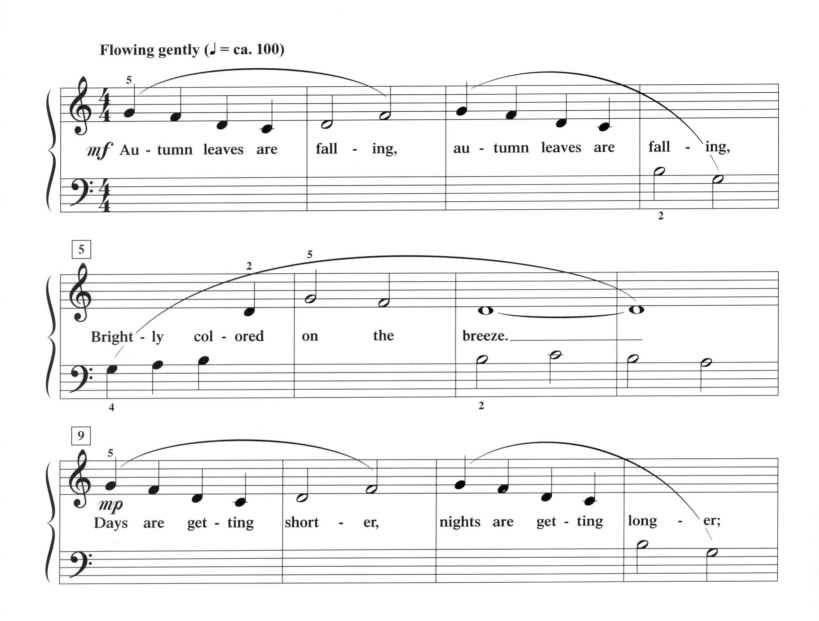

Teacher Duet: (Student plays 1 octave higher)

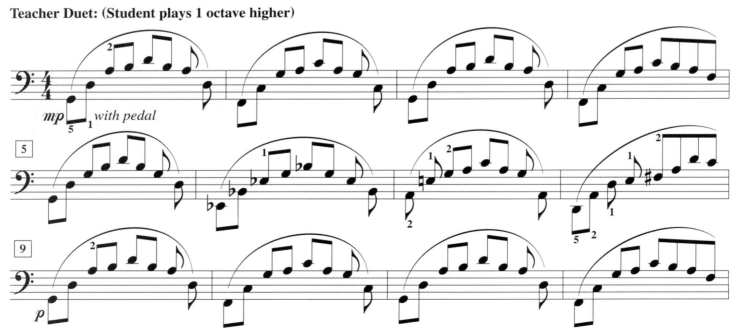

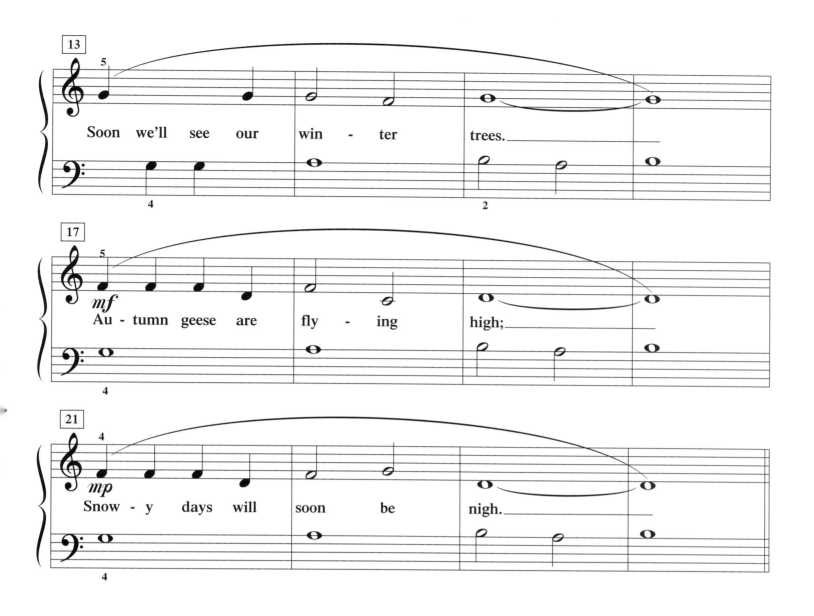